Eyes, Stones

Winner of the Walt Whitman Award for 2011

Sponsored by the Academy of American Poets, the Walt Whitman Award is given annually to the winner of an open competition among American poets who have not yet published a book of poems.

JUDGE FOR 2011: *Fanny Howe*

Poems

Eyes, Stones

Elana Bell

LOUISIANA STATE UNIVERSITY PRESS BATON ROUGE

For my grandma Zosha,
who survived—

§

Published by Louisiana State University Press

Manufactured in the United States of America
LSU Press Paperback Original
FIRST PRINTING

DESIGNER: *Mandy McDonald Scallan*
TYPEFACE: *Whitman*
PRINTER: *McNaughton & Gunn, Inc.*
BINDER: *Acme Bookbinding*

Library of Congress Cataloging-in-Publication Data

Bell, Elana, 1977–
Eyes, stones : poems / Elana Bell.
p. cm.
"LSU Press Paperback Original."
ISBN 978-0-8071-4464-0 (pbk. : alk. paper) — ISBN 978-0-8071-4466-4 (epub) — ISBN 978-0-8071-4465-7 (pdf) — ISBN 978-0-8071-4467-1 (mobi)
I. Title.
PS3602.E645448E94 2012
811'.6—dc23

2011037855

The paper in this book meets the guidelines for permanence and durability of the Committee on Production Guidelines for Book Longevity of the Council on Library Resources. ∞

Contents

Eyes, Stones

The Dream

Once in a village that burned,
before it burned, lived a young woman
who loved a young man and they waltzed
through the streets smelling of horse shit
and bread (the dogs loped behind for a scrap).

All night in separate beds they dreamed
a feast: fat wheat and cows, hills of clean soil, their hands
deep in it, and across the insides of their skulls, the name
in flaming letters, the name of the land.

When she made it there—her arms like strands of hair,
her hair in strands of rotting teeth—she could not see
her young man's face. Her after-the-war husband
seventeen years older and bald, and their daughters,
who never would have been—

I

What kind of woman goes searching and searching?
—MURIEL RUKEYSER

First Glance

Zosha and the land, 1945

you don't look what they promised
and my milk run dry   my baby scream   nothing to give her—

before God-promises   before I had a name
before soldiers or wire or guns when nothing flowered
my wet bloomed under the soil   did I choose this stone?
did I ask to be the jewel of His kingdom?

I scraped your name from my soiled sleep—
the only word   my mouth make

Wolf

Jabotinsky, 1918

Thin, my matchstick neck held
against the stable gate. The horses
inside bulged and shook the wood.
They pinned it and snarled *Jew,*
again, *Zyd,* gunning from their pipes.
A chorus of beasts, they named me
with their spit.

Once, in the brigade, I pinned a man's
throat under the heel of my boot,
his pulse quivered through the leather.
I looked down at his trembling
eyes, little rabbit, and told him
my name in the tongue of the Jew:
Ze'ev. Wolf.

How I Got My Name

Arafat

Not the one given at birth, long train
of a name that called on my father
and the Prophet in the same breath.
Not *Yasser,* meaning *no problem,*
the name I wedged into the mouth
of every politician in the Majlis,
whose prayer rugs I unfurled
five times daily like a second tongue,
same name I used to run guns
across the border into Gaza
(I never wore gloves)—

The name they whispered
in the alleys of Damascus, of Amman:
Abu Ammar, my nom de guerre. *Ammar,*
meaning *moon,* the light I captured
in a jar for rationing, meaning *immortal,*
how many lives had I stolen? We took
our children's names: *Abu Jihad,*
father of Jihad, *Abu Daoud,* of David,
Abu Ammar, for the son
I would never sire.
I wore his name like armor.

Naming the Land

Because we named the land in blood and ink
and everything held by the land
to our use   we named—
                                        dirty with the name—

Because we bought this land
when ash became sky
and the smell of burning
                                        drifted

Because my grandmother dreamed it
instead of eating death
and now new trees
grow over the graves

Because the ruined promise
because two pounds of shrapnel drawn from Noam's back
because Salim's house forced open like a jaw
a bag of pita scattered where the kitchen was

Because we can survive in any soil
because until the end of the world
we will scratch out the name

Refugee

Mordechai, Ramla, 1948

Choose a house! the captain shouted
and we scattered like rats to snatch one.
Who lived here? The doors swung
like slabs of meat on their hinges.
Inside, the cupboards gaped
to reveal their goods, stacked tight,
except a few cans rolling on the floor,
a pot on the stove still steaming.
Who lived here? I tiptoed
into the smallest room and crouched
by the foot of the bed. Mama
pulled me up and cupped my face.
Tonight you'll sleep in a proper bed
she crooned.

(the land)

come kiss the ground you dreamed—
Yes the dirt tastes like dirt

The Dig

Michalya

After it rained, my father would take me to an archaeological tell.
A whole city no one's dug up but after it rains
things come to the surface, all the little things in the ground:
shards of mosaic tile someone's clay drinking bowl
the Roman coin I shined 'til I could see my face—
And I started to fall in love with this soil;
I couldn't clean the dirt from my nails.

Oranges

Chava, 1928

What city? We were a few houses,
a street rutted out, clouded
by orchards. That smell
strangled everything.
The scent of orange and no other
sweetness could come in.

One night, a murder under the trees,
and the soil thickened.
Father grew new eyes
so he could pluck the fruit
and also watch Mother's back.
Our oranges swelled.

Tomorrow in the Apricots

Amal

They are hoping we will forget.
Forget afternoon in the cool of our courtyards, the bulbul's song
undressing the marble—
Do you forget the curl of your daughter's hair?
Or the weight of it in your hands as you braided it for school?
What about the first lie she told
looking you dead in the eye?

Charter for the Over-Sung Country

Live in me like blood,
like my name, like the numbers
tattooed on my grandmother's arm,
my mother's milk and her slow
disease. I've tried to run away.
You are not a place.
I've built a house of bricks
to keep out heavy weather.
The house falls down,
your smell comes in:
eucalyptus, salt, the goat on the altar.
I've barely undone your strap.
How long like this? I eat
your sands until I'm sick.
No one tells me: *Enough.*
All night the ram horn's wail,
the sound of you calls me
to a house that's burning.
You are not a place my love.
You come from where
there are no names. You enter
as breath and drop
onto our sleeping tongues.

You have multiplied a thousand times

Prophecy: Intifada

Michalya

No one coming. Empty buses, empty cafés.
The streets as dead as our dead boys.
And I thought, please God,
I don't want to have to tell my kids someday
about this place we used to have—
Because, for a moment, it was gone.

Kishinev

Jabotinsky, 1903

We are inside the dream of a God who's forgotten us. There is no other way to say it. Through the stippled glass I watch the neighbors hammer nails into the Jewish babies' eyes. Mama pulls me to her breasts that smell of bread and smoke. I want to look. There are no windows from which I do not see the city burning.

Letter to Jerusalem

To hold the bird and not to crush her, that is the secret. Sand turned too quickly to cement and who cares if the builders lose their arms? The musk of smoldered rats on sticks that trailed their tails through tunnels underground. Trickster of light, I walk your cobbled alleys all night long and drink your salt. City of bones, I return to you with dust on my tongue. Return to your ruined temple, your spirit of revolt. Return to you, the ache at the center of the world.

II

God's hand is in the world
like my mother's hand in the guts of the slaughtered chicken
—YEHUDA AMICHAI

God

Zosha

God is the rat-hole
where I sleep. The field

of buried potatoes. The ache
in my thighs. *Stand*

it says. *You, stand.*
If you lie down in that nest

of lice and shit, that's it—
The stomach-pain take me

from my house before
soldiers break the door.

When I come back:
everybody gone.

Mother, gone, one shoe
she drop. I want to run

after her but my leader say: *You*
don't give yourself to the enemy.

You sit put. So that's how
I survive. What do I know

from God? You hungry
mamaleh? Have a bissel soup—

What Else God Wanted

I will make the son of the maidservant into a nation also,
because he is your offspring.

—GEN. 21:13

ISHMAEL

First you were the only
and two mothers cooed
and chewed your food
to make it soft.
Then he came. The choice cut
of lamb, milk with the skein
for strength and you were told
Bring it in a silver bowl!
That was all she'd say to you,
the one who'd begged
you to be born. He smelled
like the soil after rain.
He was small enough to crush.

§

Her laugh like ankle bells,
returning from the well, a vessel
balanced on her head. Or squeezing
milk from our goats. At night
when she unbraided and brushed
my hair, her hands were like birds
and I imagined the lightness
of owning nothing. I wanted
to wear her laugh like skin,
I wanted to flood her eyes—
I sent my husband in.

§

Like sisters before
the child came.
I was the younger
and she scolded me
but when I made her laugh
I'd get my way.
And on the nights when lonely
drifted in like smoke
she'd call me to her tent.

A woman who can't bear
a child? What belongs to her?
Can I say I didn't gloat
to have a son, fat and laughing
in my lap? Of course
it all belonged to her:
the clothes, the meat, the tent.
Even the child I'd birthed. Hers
to snatch back like an angry god.

§

ABRAHAM

The morning I sent Hagar and Ishmael away,
the sun closed its eyes. Nothing shone
on the muscled back I'd oiled in the dark
of the tent, *her* back, that shouldered the skin
of water, sack of bread, our boy.
I watched until they shrank into ants
and the desert whitened.
I could have given away anything after that.

§

ISAAC

After he left I was stuck
with their desire
and their invisible god.
Father shrank and Mother paced,
counting steps like silver coins. At night
the goats circled and their bleating
filled the camp like rain.
When the one I'd helped to birth
dried up like a fig in the sun,
I brought the knife.
I filled the bowl with blood.

Bastard

The bastard brother by the well,
he will be counted. He will eat
the goat he killed. There he will plant
an olive tree. And his sons
will grow. Look at the two
brothers now:

One plunges into a pile
of rotted shoes. No feet inside.
The other holds a detonator.
He will pull the cord and explode
suffering into hunks:
something to be eaten.

Visiting Auschwitz

what extra scrap of bread
what glance from a slop-drunk SS

what rage raised the rusted shovel
struck it on the starving ground

until the whistle ended day
what muscle corded in the thighs

not buckling to the bed of lice of bloody flux
what propped her up when her bowels released

the spoiled cabbage soup and she couldn't hold
her dead-weight head what switched the names

so she was not called what
scarf smuggled from the storage hull

a shred so she could wipe herself
what song muffled in the dark

what glint willed the breath
what saw her and said *live*

How I Got My Name

Jabotinsky

All night, under the moon's bulging
eye, my mother walked, one hand
on her belly, one on the knife
she'd slipped from the kitchen.

She heard the wolf before she saw
it, dragging its catch by the rump
into the clearing. The animal raised
its muzzle to the moon and urged
the pups out from the pines.

My mother watched them feast
on that dead deer—its bones
gleamed like pearls. She dropped
the knife and buried it there, the wolves
gazing with their sleepy, yellowed eyes.

The Chairman

Arafat, 1939

From the time I was ten, instead of school,
I lined up the neighborhood boys, made them
march our narrow streets. If one
stepped out of line or disobeyed,
I whacked him with a stick.

The men with oiled beards
and kaffiyehs laughed from inside
their tiny shops. *Little dictator* they called
through the shisha smoke. They watched
with glittering eyes. Then gestured me inside.

Homeland: A Fable

Michalya

They are the trees and we are the birds.
The birds have conquered the trees.
Now we're saying to the trees:
We were trees before you were trees.
And the trees are saying: *Well,*
you're birds now. You've been birds
for a really long time. And
you're shitting on us.

Notes from the Broken Notebook

(part one)

and it is certain as I write this, another house bulldozed,
    another army order
arms reaching from the trunk of her body
awakened at sunrise by the call to prayer, *for what do we pray?*
cover your mouth, you'll still inhale the gas
dance in the shadow of the concrete wall
    tell yourself the tiles are not bones
even in a dream you must still make choices
fill the guest's cup three times before he gives the news
five fingers, the same hand
flour sacks piled to hold back the flood
gather the ghosts of the asylum built on top of a village
helplessness worn like an invisible necklace
her wail fills the streets like a siren:
    noon and the whole city stops
hold the two stones like children to my breast
if you have no language you have nothing
I have lost the tape of my grandmother's words
I want to meet a Palestinian—an exotic bird on my tongue
keys to a house you will never see again
my grandfather danced like his feet were on fire
no hope, *know hope*
not a house, pieces of a house
only free men can negotiate
pink fleshy sky and our faces disappear
return to the satisfaction of chopping vegetables,
    the same in any country
stop speaking—you have no words for this
the broken doll in the courtyard, its eyes still rolling

the woman covers her face with a siddur, raises it to the sky
white cranes dip their beaks into the dead sheep
    and feast
today I will tell her I'm a Jew
we make many children so that if some are killed . . .

what privileges the eye?
who decides what survives?

The Weakest One

Zosha

A little meat, they keep
you for work. All day

the sun beating
into our skin, spoiling

our brains. We sang
songs, we ate air.

The guard couldn't put us
together, so she went

to get someone higher up
to beat us. I was skinny

but I could make order.
I marched those girls

into line. I saved our crusts
and hid them like gold.

What did I have?
A little meat. A song

my father used to sing
about a place we could go—

Except my brother in Israel
I was the only one

who survived. And I
was the weakest one.

Naming Our Dead

Alma. al-Ashrafiyya. Abu Shusha. Ajjur. Artuf. Abramowo.
al-Bassa. al-Bira. Babiak. Bayt Jirja. Belz. Bialystock. Bi'ina.
Biriyya. Burkanow. al-Baqqara. Busk. Braslow. Chmielnik.
Chodorow. Chomsk. al-Damun. Danna. Deir Yassin.
Dimra. al-Dirdara. Dolzka. Dvinsk. Druja.
Dworzec. Dubno. Ejszyszeki. Filipow. Fir'im.
Farwana. al-Faluja. al-Fatur. Grodek.
Grodno. Gdansk. Ghajar. al-Ghazzawaiyya.
Golina. Glinki. Horodek. Hajnowka. al-Hamra.
al-Hiquab. Harrawi. al-Husayniyya. al-Hindaj. Ilnik. Ilintsky.
Indur. Iqrit. Ijzim. Jaroslaw. Jurze. Jahula. Jabbul. Jazayir.
Jedwabne. Jadow. Jubb Yusef. Janowiec. Kabara. Kafr Bir-
im. al-Khisas. Kirrad. Kulikow. Korzec.
Khubbayza. Koropiec. Krynki. Korolowka.
Kafr'Ana. Lesko. Lobzenica. Lutomiersk.
Lifta. al-Lajjun. al-Lydd. Lysiec. Ludmir. Lubya.
Ma'lul. al-Mansura. al-Mazar.Mielnik. Mezhirech.
Mughallis. al-Mirr. Myslowice. Miedzno. Mogilno. Nitaf.
Nowogrodek. Nadworna. Niebylec. Nawaqir. al-Nahr.
Nuris. Ostrozec. Obryzycko. Oslakow. Ostryna. al-
Omour. Piatkowa. Piaski. Plonsk. Pryzybyszew.
Qumya. Qisarya. Quannir. Qira. Radzilow.
Rudki. Rantiya Ras Abu'Amar. Rejowic.
Rakow. Rogozhin. Sambor. Stawaski. Sabbarin.
Saqiya. Sniadowo. Strzeliska. Sha'ab. Sirin. Turze.
Trembowla. Tarnow. Tarbikha. Ustrzykie. Ulanow. Umm.
al-Shawf. Warenz. Wizna. Wadi'Ara. Wojnilow. al-Walaja.
Yajur. Yubla.Yaquq. Zabludow. Zir'in. Zarnuqa. al-Zeeb.

On a Hilltop at the Nassar Farm

overlooking the settlement of Neve Daniel

This is for Amal, whose name means *hope,*
who thinks of each tree she's planted like a child,
whose family has lived in the same place
for a hundred years, and when I say place
I mean this exact patch of land
where her father was born, and his father,
so that the shoots he planted before her birth
now sweep over her head. Every March
she plucks the green almonds and chews
their sour fuzzy husks like medicine.

I have never stayed anywhere long enough
to plant something and watch it settle into its bloom.
I am from a people who move,
who crossed sea and desert and city
with stone monuments, with clocks, with palaces
on foot, on skeleton trains, through barracks
with iron bunks, aching for a place we could stay.
All our prayers, all our songs for that place
where we had taken root once, where we had been
the ones to send the others packing and now—

Amal laughs with all her teeth and her feet
tickle the soil when she walks. She moves
through her land like an animal. She knows it
in the dark. She feeds stalks to the newborn
colt and collects its droppings like coins
to fertilize the field. Amal loves this land
and when I say land I mean this
exact dirt and the fruit of it

and the sheep who graze it and the children
who eat from it and the dogs who protect it
and the tiny white blossoms it scatters in spring.

And when I say love I mean Amal has never married.

All around her land the settlements sprout like weeds.
They block out the sun and suck precious water
through taps and pipes while Amal digs wells
to collect the rain. I am writing this poem
though I have never drunk rain
collected from a well dug by my own hands,
never pulled a colt through
the narrow opening covered in birth fluid
and watched its mother lick it clean,
or eaten a meal made entirely of things
I got down on my knees to plant.

And when I say settlement I mean
I love the red tiled roofs,
the garden in the shape of a garden,
water that comes when I call it forth
with the flick of my wrist and my hand on the tap.
Only lately I find that when I ache
it takes the shape of a well.
And when I bleed I emit a scent
something like a sheep in heat,
like dirt after rain,
like a patch of small white flowers
too wild to name.

III

My country is not a suitcase
I am not a traveler
I am the lover and the land is the beloved.
—MAHMOUD DARWISH

Flags

Everywhere, in the fertile soil of this land,
we've planted flags. Flags sprout like the hair
from an old man's nostrils. Blue and white
or red, black, green, and white, they shroud
windows, standing in for a family
you can't see: a flag instead of the mother
who hums and spices the lentils, a flag
for Father, who runs the blade against his cheek
each morning with the rooster's *kukuku*.
Later, in the dark, he holds his wife
while the children sleep wrapped in flags.
Flags grow in the garden, flags from the beaks
of muted birds. Shredded flags drape phone wires,
flags hang from the pines like dead hands—

The Key

He felt for his key the way he would feel for
his limbs and was reassured.

—MAHMOUD DARWISH

In the old ones with rot-mouth lingers the key.
The boy lost his fingers, his mouth sings the key.

A split pomegranate shines in the crack of her palm.
Under seed, in the pulp of its rind, glints the key.

Loai al Lahawane, twenty-two years old:
A bomb belts his waist, around his neck swings the key.

From the limbs of our dead boy flourished an oak.
And now in his memory we name King—the key!

This longing you whisper through concrete and wire,
Which crumbling building returned brings the key?

A village wedding, cement blocks line the field.
Around the bride's rusted finger—no ring—the key.

The girl with caramel cheeks shrieks and chases our bus,
Her uncoiled six-year-old arms shrink the key.

All day we settle olive shoots in impossible soil,
Palms pocked and red-stained—is suffering the key?

Around Har Hakarmel the lush land pulses—
From a peak above the city a bird flings the key.

Climb into the pliable cave of my body,
In the shadow of its unfolded wing, the key.

Letter to Hebron

I want to write you and not the dream of you. Write your stones that smell of chalk and piss. There they are again, those fucking stones. What else can I name? The goat head strung like a lantern from your market stall, flies crowding its open eyes. And on the flat overlooking Kiryat Arba, the boy with paper shoes who circled his mule then whipped him with a branch until he bucked and stood on two legs like a man—his teeth, his shame. That wooden doorway, hung without a house.

Notes from the Broken Notebook

(part two)

bag of pita still warm
boy with a rubber bullet in his palm
breeze lifts the heat

brown palm, and the rubber coating red
bulldozer suspended, at rest on the Sabbath
carob drying on the branch

copper pot for boiling the coffee
cup that held the tea
dead sheep on its side

dog following me
dog without a name in the language I speak
eerie yellow dust coats the air

field with holes where the trees were transported
girl sings and picks at her skin
girl with no brothers left

girl with rivers for eyes
goat-head (open eyes) hung from the stall
graveyard with graves for beds

house that is no longer a house
jasmine bush blooming over the dumpster—
　　　　the smell of jasmine forgets the war

Jew in a black fur hat
Jew in a tank top and spiked heels
knife carves two names into cactus flesh

mother holds her baby in the crowded market
mother bends and plants tomatoes in the shattered greenhouse
mother hurls herself on her son's wooden box

paste made from dates to sweeten the morning
plastic chair hangs in a dusty olive tree
prayer callus on his forehead like the thumbprint of God

Catalogue

Jabotinsky

A copy of the Torah, its leather cover worn thin; three rifles, two pistols, two hundred and fifty rounds of ammunition; a selection of silk ties organized by color, nothing too bright or showy; a wooden Philco radio; silver pocket watch engraved; a bottle of aftershave imported from France. The photograph of one-armed Trumpledor; black spectacles, no case; a badge of the Members of the British Empire, sterling, strung on a red silk ribbon, encased in glass.

Visiting Aida refugee camp

a conversation with ghosts

today I cannot tell truth from lie
bone from milk
my grandmother's words from ash:

someone has left a cherry stone in the path
when we were small we played marbles
with the dead rats' eyes we marked
where we hid our hearts so someone
could find them and stuff them
into the birds we longed to be

my grandmother's face from milk
truth from ash
a stone from my fist:

someone has left an iron key under my pillow
at night I press cool metal to my cheek
its open eye knows all the doors
that used to sing in Arabic
this key won't break or rot
like my hand my eye

In Another Country It Could Have Been Love

Walid

When her fingers swooped in like wrens
to pluck the fattest dates
from Father's bin and lay them
on the scale, I wanted
to kiss those quick brown hands.

The next time I saw her, a rifle
strapped her shoulder. The tip
of it fingered my ribs, my hips,
the inside of my thighs.
Cold metal instead of her hands,
her eyes.

Treaty with Jordan

Michalya

That night, riding home on the only road
between Jerusalem and Hebron,
when traffic froze and one man unfurled his kaffiyeh
like a flag, when almond blossoms rained
instead of stones on the bulletproof glass of our bus,
I *saw.*

There Are Things This Poem Would Rather Not Say:

We ate labneh and bread in your tents

When we had no water
          we drew it from your well

Your camels carried the sand to build our houses
          you built them—your hands—

Fig-tree   prickly-pear   human-flood

You were the wasteland we made bloom

Military Tactics

Arafat, 1968

They wanted us to wait. Wait for a Saladin to rise and save us from the sewers of Egypt, of Jordan. Who would come? When I blew up that first water pump I stayed to watch the Jewish plants and seeds swept into the flood, their shriveled roots clutching at the sky. The night before they invaded Karameh I told the smallest one: No one to save us but us.

Letter to Arafat

In the rebuilt café where the bride exploded with the glass, we order cappuccino to sip with our cigarettes. Across the invisible line, only Arabic coffee. In Gaza they make rockets from lead pipe and nails. We say animals. Is a body worth a body? What if it has wept in the rain? Whispered the ninety-nine names of God? In the first light. Before morning.

Inheritance

Amal

Under Turkish rule
we bought this land.
After, the British came
and we stayed
in caves,
preparing the soil.
Then the Jordanians,
and we planted
olive shoots and almond seeds.
Now the Jews.
We haven't left yet.
We pluck the fruit
before it falls.
When the Palestinians
come to power, we'll be
right here, harvesting
our olives, pressing
for oil.

Language in the Mouth of the Enemy

I am afraid that this poem
will contribute to the destruction of Israel.
I am afraid that if I visit Adel Handal and his family
in Bethlehem one more time
I am betraying the Jewish state.
If I go to Daher's Vineyard and plant an olive tree,
if I teach the women of Nahalin poetry,
if I give voice to their rage,
what great-aunt of mine shot in the back
before an unmarked grave will have died then,
again for nothing?
If I love the suffering of the Palestinians—it is so bright—
more than the suffering of my own,
if I work for a better life for that dark-eyed boy
in Aida refugee camp who chased after our bus with arms
spread like a hawk's wing-span—who lifted a finger
to save the child in Warsaw, Lodz, Berlin?—
If that boy grows strong and straps a bomb
or worse, writes an article, a play, the perfect
argument against the Jewish state
then what have I done? What have I
done? What have
I done?

(the land)

before you came and before and before that—
they trickled in

like the salt that formed the rock
in tents in mud huts under the ledge

where the goat-keep grazed his goats
or his father's goats

on weeds on fallen almonds
olive milk

and by the monthly moon
the wet knot of animal

undone into the fire
into the dust swept by wind

in the night
little man fires—

Letter to Brooklyn

When I come home to you, I'll watch the Super Bowl. I'll buy waterproof boots if it rains and sheepskin gloves for my cold hands. I'll eat organic greens and make love on Saturday afternoon when no one is in a rush. I'll listen to jazz in a tight-packed club with red lipstick on to tease the man behind the bar. I'll sigh about the candidates for president—*it's all hot air*—but clench a secret hope, so secret I'm not even sure it's there. And at night, after a glass of wine and the internet, I will sleep on clean cotton sheets—In my dreams there's a knock on the wind. Someone drags me from my feast and paints a mask of open sky over my eyes, then ropes my wrists and ties me to a tree. I twist but I can't fly. And no one comes to save me.

§

Your Village

Once in a village that is burning
    because a village is always somewhere burning

And if you do not look because it is not your village
    it is still your village

In that village is a hollow child
    You drown when he looks at you with his black, black eyes

And if you do not cry because he is not your child
    he is still your child

All the animals that could run away have run away
    The trapped ones make an orchestra of their hunger

The houses are ruin   Nothing grows in the garden
    The grandfather's grave is there   a small stone

under the shade of a charred oak   Who will brush off the dead
    leaves   Who will call his name for morning prayer

Where will they—the ones who slept in this house and ate from this dirt—?

Notes

"Wolf"—Jabotinsky was a Revisionist Zionist leader who preached widely throughout Europe from the early 1900s until his death in 1940. He helped form the Jewish Legion in the British army during World War I.

"How I Got My Name (*Arafat*)"—*Majlis* refers to the Egyptian parliament. Abu Ammar, Abu Daoud, and Abu Jihad were the names taken by Arafat and other key members of Fatah early on in the Palestinian national movement.

"Refugee"—In 1948, during the Arab-Israeli War, tens of thousands of Ramla's Arab residents fled or were expelled. The town was subsequently repopulated by Jewish immigrants.

"Oranges"—In the early days of Jewish immigration to Palestine, there were occasional outbreaks of violence between neighboring Jewish and Arab communities.

"Tomorrow in the Apricots"—The title is a translation of an Arabic phrase, *Bukra fil mish mish,* which is equivalent to the saying "It'll never happen." The bulbul is a bird often referred to in Arabic poetry, known for its song.

"Kishinev"—The Kishinev pogrom took place in 1903. It entailed three days of violent rioting against the Jews, who were falsely accused of murdering a Christian boy.

"God"—*Bissel* is the Yiddish word for "a little bit of." *Mamaleh* is a Yiddish term of endearment.

"Naming Our Dead" is a composite of Jewish villages and communities in eastern Europe destroyed or made "Jew-free" during World War II, as well as Palestinian villages destroyed or evacuated in 1948 during the Arab-Israeli War.

"The Key"—Palestinian refugees often carry the keys to their ancestral homes in Israel. Har Hakarmel is a mountain in the north of Israel.

"Letter to Hebron"—Kiryat Arba is a Jewish settlement in Hebron.

"Catalogue"—Joseph Trumpeldor was an early Zionist activist who died defending the settlement of Tel Hai in 1920. His last words were, "Never mind, it is good to die for our country."

"Treaty with Jordan"—On October 26, 1994, Israel made peace with Jordan. Palestinians and Israelis, Arabs and Jews, took to the streets in celebration.

"Military Tactics"—Karameh is a town in Jordan, and was the battleground for one of the main events in the history of the Palestinian national movement in 1968.

"Language in the Mouth of the Enemy"—Nahalin is a Palestinian village in the West Bank, near Bethlehem.

Acknowledgments

I would like to thank the editors of the following publications, in which the poems listed first appeared, sometimes in earlier versions: *CALYX:* "On a Hilltop at the Nassar Farm"; *Hanging Loose:* "Visiting Auschwitz"; *Harvard Review:* "The Key"; *Massachusetts Review:* "Your Village"; *Mima'amakim:* "Refugee"; *Southern Poetry Review:* "How I Got My Name (Jabotinsky)"; *Storyscape:* "The Dream"; *Union Station:* "Charter for the Over-Sung Country." "On a Hilltop at the Nassar Farm" also appeared in the anthology *Before There Is Nowhere to Stand* (Lost Horse Press, 2012). "Flags," "Letter to Arafat," "Letter to Jerusalem," "Naming the Land," and "There are things this poem would rather not say" first appeared online at www.poets.org from the Academy of American Poets.

§

I am grateful to the Jerome Foundation, the Edward Albee Foundation, and the Drisha Institute for their generous support during the making of this book.

I send deep and profound thanks to the many people—family, friends, and teachers—who have made this book possible. In particular I would like to thank Fanny Howe, Suzanne Gardinier, Laure-Anne Bosselaar, Naomi Shihab Nye, John Easterly, Catherine Kadair, and everyone at LSU Press, Kate Quarfordt for her beautiful cover image, Mimi Schownwald, and the Schownwald family, Elana Rozenman, George Rishmawi, Aracelis Girmay, Pat Rosal, Samantha Thornhill, Lynne Procope, Gabrielle Calvocoressi, Pamela Samuelson, Abena Koomson, Laura Marie Thompson, Benj Kamm, Melissa Weintraub, and Ilana Sumka. To the following organizations that have been instrumental in supporting me as an artist and educator, I also offer my appreciation: Bronx Academy of Letters, Community Word Project, Elders Share the Arts, and the LouderARTS Project.

I would especially like to acknowledge the Palestinians and Israelis who opened their homes and shared their lives with me—I am changed because of you. And to the many organizations in Israel and Palestine working tirelessly for a just peace, you are a light: Seeds of Peace, Encounter, Just Vision, Tent of Nations, Neve Shalom/Wahat al Salaam, Jerusalem Peacemakers, Holy Land Trust, and Siraj, the Center for Holy Land Studies.

Endless gratitude to my parents, Phil and Chana Bell, who have always encouraged me to follow my inner voice, and to my brother Michael, who has taught me so much about listening. To Frieda, John, Danny, Joey, Brian, Jeremy, Inhee, and Cara, thank you for being such a loving family. And to the Chakrabartis, who welcomed me with open arms.

And finally, to my husband, Jai, for your careful reading and tireless support. Your love opens every door.